the color of my soul

a self-portrait in words

A Guided Journal

By Lynn Rosen
Illustrated by Steve Haskamp

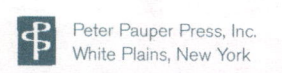

Peter Pauper Press, Inc.
White Plains, New York

This journal belongs to _____

Designed by Lesley Ehlers
Cover design by Heather Zschock

Illustrations copyright © 2001 Steve Haskamp

Text copyright © 2001
Peter Pauper Press, Inc.
202 Mamaroneck Avenue
White Plains, NY 10601
All rights reserved
ISBN 0-88088-264-6
Printed in China

7 6 5 4 3 2 1

Visit us at www.peterpauper.com

The Coloring Book of Life

You're so angry, you see **red.** Feeling jealous? You're **green** with envy. A bit down in the dumps? You've got the **blues**.

Colors are often used to express how we feel. In fact, colors, according to scientists and psychologists, not only express our emotions, but influence them as well. The colors in our world affect how we feel and how others see us.

Color can also tell us something about ourselves, our personalities, our dominant characteristics—and our souls. The many colors of our souls encompass the rich range of hues that make up the rainbow—each color with its own unique meaning.

We seek to know ourselves, and to understand our fundamental natures. The search for meaning and self-knowledge is an ongoing, often challenging, often fulfilling journey. Enrich this journey with color, and discover the color of your soul.

The Color of My Soul journal is designed to help you learn more about yourself through color. It provides information about the essence of different colors, and asks questions to guide you through an exploration of what various colors represent in your life.

We have many different colors in us, some stronger than others, each reflecting a different aspect of ourselves. Use this journal to learn your own true colors.

L. R.

Explanatory Notes

This journal is divided into sections about the seven colors of the spectrum: red, orange, yellow, green, blue, indigo, and violet. It also includes black and white, both of which contain the entire spectrum within them. Each of these colors tells us something different about ourselves.

Every section contains questions about personal qualities that are related to the particular color. In answering the questions, write as well about other thoughts or memories that come to mind. Also throughout this journal, you will find information about the following:

Chakras

A *chakra*, meaning wheel in Sanskrit, is an energy center in your body. The chakras derive from ancient Indian yoga tradition. There are seven major chakras, and each one corresponds to one of the seven colors of the rainbow.

Color Therapy

Color therapy, like the chakras, is rooted in ancient tradition. This practice believes that certain parts of our bodies correspond to certain colors, and that various ailments and problems can be cured with the proper application of color.

The Zodiac

The signs of the Zodiac also have color associations. Some signs have aspects of more than one color in them, so you will find them in more than one section of the journal. The back of the journal has a chart listing all the signs of the Zodiac and their corresponding dates.

Pictures

Each section has space at the end for a picture in that color. Interpret this however you like. Paste in a picture of yourself wearing that color. Use a crayon or marker in that color and draw an original picture. Or cut something out of a magazine that is in the color of the section, or represents something associated with that color.

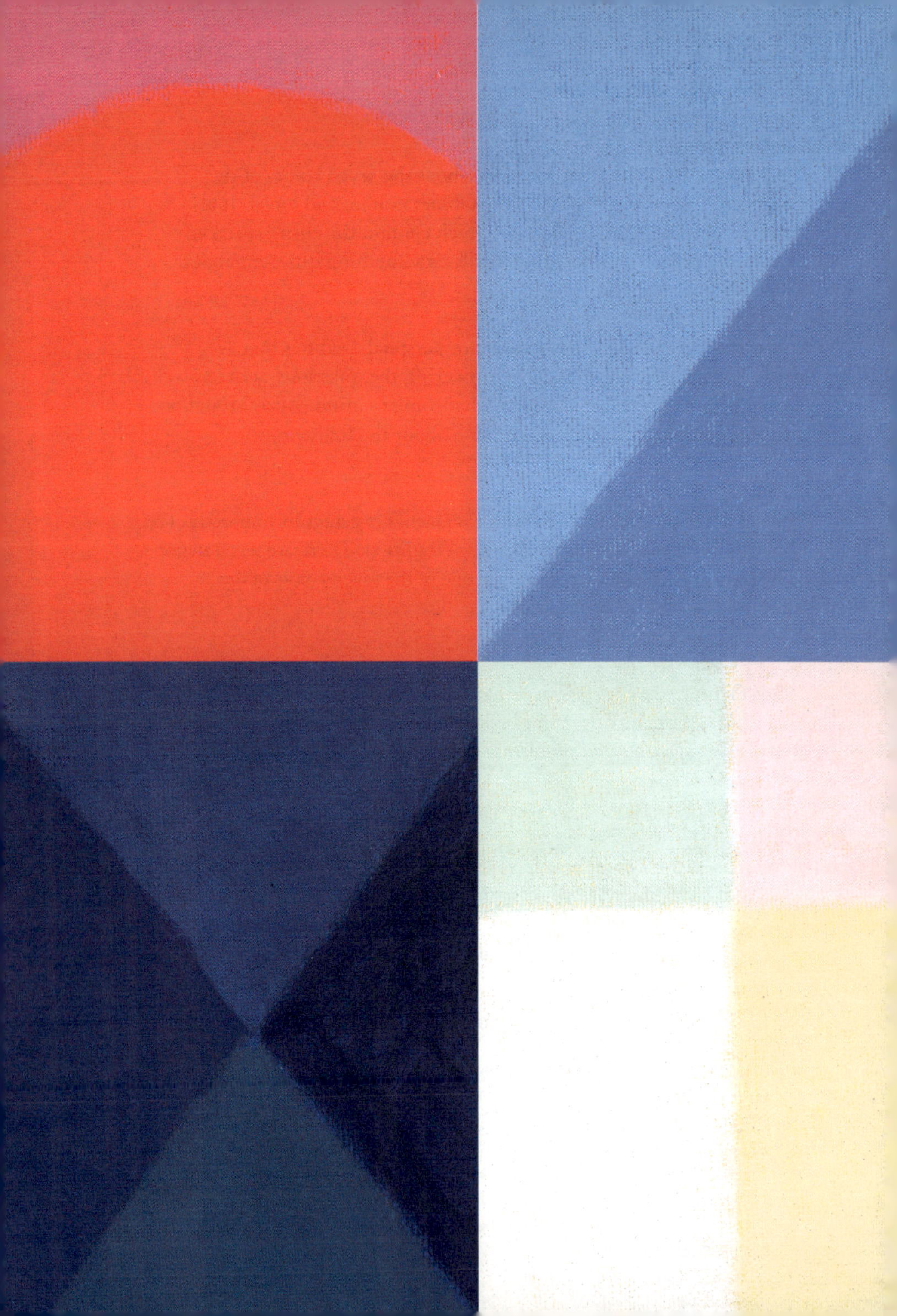

red **9**

orange **27**

yellow **45**

green **63**

blue **81**

indigo **99**

violet **117**

black **135**

white 149

The red chakra is located at the base of your spine. Associated with the element earth, this "root" chakra is concerned with survival and material security. It is also connected to stability and a desire to achieve goals.

What are your great passions?

Red gemstones
ruby, garnet, red spinel

The Zodiac

Aries' color is a vivid scarlet. Libra is associated with soft pinks and Scorpio with bright ruby red.

Do you think of yourself as a successful person? Why or why not?

Color therapy
Red can give you courage and confidence and renew your energy.

A Red Picture

orange

Orange vibrates with joy. Orange lightens our minds, enabling us to experience the energy of our physical beings. Orange can be restless, anxious; orange wants to go places.

Orange is a vocal color, never one to fade into the background. Orange is the color of the dawn, of beginnings. Orange has a childish spontaneity, a glee for life.

Does orange spark your soul?

Color therapy
Orange makes you feel joyful and energetic, and removes your inhibitions.

How do you best express yourself physically? Dancing? Sports? Sex? Are you comfortable with your body?

Orange is the "spleen" chakra, located below the navel. Its element is water. This chakra is associated with sex and other primal feelings. It is also tied in to a need to love and be loved, and to personal creativity.

Do you have a lot of energy? Do you get restless?
How do you deal with these feelings?

Orange gemstones
topaz, coral, carnelian

The Zodiac
Leo is associated with warm orange tones.

Have you started something new lately—a job, a relationship, a project? How does it feel to begin again?

An Orange Picture

yellow

Yellow is the color of the mind, of intellectual pursuits. Bright as the sun, yellow seeks enlightenment.

Also like the sun, yellow has heat—the warmth of an engaging personality and a fun-loving spirit. Yellow throws a party and dances 'til dawn. Yellow is exuberant.

Yellow is expressive and communicative.

Does your soul express itself in yellow?

Are you good at expressing your feelings? Are you a better talker or a listener?

Yellow gemstones
yellow sapphire, citrine

The Zodiac
Gemini is lemon yellow, Leo golden. Scorpio can be deep yellow.

How do you satisfy your intellectual curiosity?

Color therapy
Yellow cheers you up and makes you think more clearly.

The yellow chakra is action-oriented. Located at the solar plexus, it is connected to the element fire and to personal power. A sense of identity, and self-esteem, authority, and self-control—all are related to this chakra.

What's your idea of fun on a free day or evening?

A Yellow Picture

green

Green is at the center of the color spectrum, and hence represents balance. It is a healing color. Green is about caring and helping.

Green is the color of growth, and will point you toward new directions in your life.

Green invokes the lushness of nature. Imagine yourself deep in the woods after a rain, walking a path overhung with a thick canopy of wet leaves, protective, enveloping, mysterious.

Is your soul balanced by green?

Green gemstones
emerald, jade, malachite, tourmaline

How would you change your life if you could?

The green chakra is the heart chakra. This middle chakra is all about love. It unifies the opposites of male and female, and mind and body. The heart chakra represents harmony, forgiveness, and compassion.

The Zodiac

The Cancer sign is linked with green. Other signs have various green tints, Capricorn being dark green, Aquarius pale green, and Pisces, of course, sea green.

Do you feel that your life is in balance?
What makes it so, or what needs to change to bring it into balance?

Have you ever suffered illness, either physical or mental? What helped you heal?

Color therapy

Green soothes your nerves and brings a feeling of peace and harmony.

A Green Picture

blue

Blue is the color of peace, of meditative calm. Inspiring reflection, blue is a decisive color.

The blue of the Madonna's robes is the blue of devotion. Baby blue is the color of commitment. Powder blue speaks in the gentlest of tones of wide open spaces and possibility.

We stretch our legs and fold our arms beneath our heads, and lie back to contemplate a full blue sky, lush with clouds and ripe with sunshine—a wide open space in which thoughts and dreams can soar.

Is blue reflected in your soul?

What could you do to make your life less stressful?
Where is your favorite place to relax?

Blue is the throat chakra. It relates to self-expression and communication. The blue chakra connects to truth and integrity.

How do you behave in a crisis?

Blue gemstones
aquamarine, turquoise

Are you at peace with yourself? Why or why not?

The Zodiac

Blue is a popular color in the Zodiac. Taurus is a light blue sign. Gemini is slate blue, while Virgo is navy. Libra is sky blue and Aquarius takes the hue of electric blue.

Color therapy
Blue will calm you down and make you sleep. Blue makes you feel connected.

A Blue Picture

Indigo

Indigo has a vivid imagination, seeing what others may not be able to see. Indigo is intuitive, and soaks up new information easily. Indigo is uninhibited and receptive to new ways of thinking.

Indigo believes in universal harmony, and is devoted to loved ones. Indigo will try to heal the world.

Indigo is bluer than blue. It is the color of mystery, where the sky meets the night. Indigo is a veil draped across a face, leaving only the eyes exposed, searching, probing, seeking to fathom the great unknown.

Does indigo inspire your soul?

Imagine yourself lying on the beach and staring off into the sky or into the surf. What occupies your thoughts?

___

Indigo gemstones
sapphire, lapis lazuli, iolite

Color therapy

Indigo will soothe mental anxiety and release your fears. Indigo opens your mind and helps you to communicate more clearly.

The Indigo chakra is at the brow. This "forehead chakra" is often referred to as the "third eye." This imaginary third eye will help you detect falsehoods and deceit.

Are you an intuitive person, or do you look for hard evidence?

Do others come to you for help? Do you enjoy helping others?

The Zodiac
Sagittarius is a deep indigo blue.

An Indigo Picture

violet

Violet is a highly spiritual color. It is the color of truth. Violet provides insight, and violet inspires us to strive for a higher purpose.

Violet has strong intuition and great faith. Follow violet to the soul's interior.

Once reserved for royalty, violet is a regal color. Wear violet and you will stand tall, you will be noticed.

Is your soul enlightened by violet?

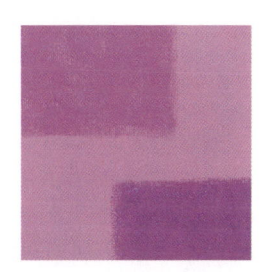

The Zodiac
Sagittarius is a vivid violet.

Violet gemstone
Amethyst

Do you have a spiritual side? If so, how does it manifest itself?

Are you always striving for something better? If so, how?

The crown chakra is violet. This is the most spiritual chakra. It signifies unity and integration, as well as wisdom and purpose. When it is developed, this chakra brings fulfillment and bliss.

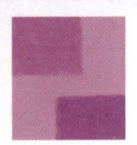

What do you think makes you special?

Color therapy

Violet enhances your creativity, strengthens your values, and helps clear up emotional problems.

A Violet Picture

black

Black is strong and firm. Black has no doubts. Black has courage and knows how to persevere.

Black can be protective, like the black of night. Black is authoritative, for it cannot be overcome. Yet black can be soft and mellow and flexible. With the grace of a cat, black can mold itself to any situation.

Black can soar with the wings of a bird and find footing in any territory.

Does black stand firm in your soul?

Color therapy

Black is compatible with silence, and the state of calm that is brought on by silent meditation. Black invokes discipline, independence, and strength of will.

Do you consider yourself a strong person? What makes you feel strong?

What makes you afraid?

Black gemstones
black opal, onyx, ebony, jet

The Zodiac

Gemini is a pale grey, Virgo a deeper grey. Capricorn is granite grey. Scorpio is black.

Do you feel responsible for your family and friends? Why?

A Black Picture

white

Pure and unsullied, white is without color, compatible and yet separate.

White strives for peace and works with others, yet stands firm in its own beliefs. White flows, yet sets boundaries. White can mix with any color and bring about change, whether subtle or dramatic.

Serene and calm, white is respectful and quiet, but white never fades.

Does white pacify your soul?

Are you argumentative or do you avoid conflict?
How do you react when others argue in your presence?

Color therapy

White, the color of purity, will help you renew yourself and feel ready to begin again.

Do you get along with many different types of people, or do you prefer to be with people with whom you have much in common? Do you blend into a crowd, or do you like to be the star?

White gemstones
pearl, diamond

Are you confident in your opinions and beliefs, or are you easily swayed?

The Zodiac

Aries
March 21 ▪ April 19

Taurus
April 20 ▪ May 20

Gemini
May 21 ▪ June 20

Cancer
June 21 ▪ July 22

Leo
July 23 ▪ August 22

Virgo
August 23 ▪ September 22

Libra
September 23 ▪ October 22

Scorpio
October 23 ▪ November 21

Sagittarius
November 22 ▪ December 21

Capricorn
December 22 ▪ January 19

Aquarius
January 20 ▪ February 18

Pisces
February 19 ▪ March 20